Red Grooms

Essay by
Thomas Micchelli

Photography by
Peter Sumner Walton Bellamy

Marlborough

Copyright © 2021 Marlborough Gallery
545 West 25th Street
New York, New York 10001
Telephone (212) 541 4900

First Edition: 1000 copies

Edited by Marissa Jade Moxley

Book design by Dana Martin-Strebel

Typset: Baskerville

Copyright© 2021 Essay by Thomas Micchelli
Copyright © 2021 Photography by Peter Sumner Walton Bellamy

Cover photo by Rudy Burckhardt, 1981
© 2021 Estate of Rudy Burckhardt / Artists Rights Society (ARS), New York

Printed in China by Permanent Printing Limited
ISBN: 978-0-89797-142-3

Table of Contents

Looking at Red Grooms

Thomas Micchelli

Temple of Athena, Parthenon, Nashville, TN

Red Grooms, *Walking the Dogs*, 1981 (detail)

Red Grooms's first trip to the Temple of Athena, Goddess of Wisdom, didn't go very well:

> Some people speak of the "horror vacui" in my work. I believe it stems from a childhood experience when I was led by the hand through the great bronze door into the empty interior space of Nashville's Parthenon. I remember screaming and running away. A horrible void; I just couldn't stand it.[1]

His relationship with the goddess improved years later when, as a young man, he visited the same building to take in a traveling exhibition organized by the American Federation of Arts, where he laid eyes on Jackson Pollock's dreamlike *Sleeping Effort* (1953), a swirling convergence of chunky shapes and rich, deep color. As Judd Tully wrote in *Smithsonian Magazine* (June 1, 1985), "For Grooms it was an epiphany. At this point he decided to pursue 'fine art.'"[2]

Jackson Pollock, *Sleeping Effort*, 1953
oil and enamel on canvas
49 7/8 x 76 in. / 126.7 x 193 cm
University purchase, Bixby Fund, 1954 WU 3842 © 2021
The Pollock-Krasner Foundation / Artists Rights Society
(ARS), New York.

The Pollock, now in The Mildred Lane Kemper Art Museum of Washington University in St. Louis, is an unsettled, unsettling transitional work. Completed three years before the artist's death, it feels caught between his abstract, landscape-inflected drip technique and the evocatively figurative brushwork of his last paintings, though no less all-over in its compositional approach.

In 1963, ten years after Pollock painted *Sleeping Effort*, Grooms landed in New York City after a series of peripatetic escapades, all in pursuit of fine art — from the School of the Art Institute of Chicago to the George Peabody College for Teachers in Nashville; from New York's New School for Social Research to Hans Hofmann's studio in Provincetown, Massachusetts — gathering friends, ideas, and adventures along the way.

This was the moment when he made his first "stick outs" — artworks "[h]overing at the boundary between painting and sculpture," as Judith E. Stein described them.[3]

"I started making 'stick outs' early in 1963," Grooms told her in an interview, "after spending a year making movie sets. We talked a lot about '3-D-ing.'"[4]

Originally invented out of necessity — an "experience," he continued, "of working frantically in thick muddy paint, losing the whole thing and using cardboard glued in quickly to regain a clearer image"[5] — the "stick out" was the acorn that grew into the colossal "sculpto-pictorama" of *Ruckus Manhattan* a dozen years later.[6]

The movie sets he mentioned were built for *Shoot the Moon* (1962), the 24-minute, 16mm, DIY short he made with Rudy Burckhardt and Mimi Gross, based on Georges Méliès's silent classic, *A Trip to the Moon* (1902). By this time, Grooms had already done a stint working as a uniformed usher, complete with gloves and epaulets, at New York's cavernous Roxy Theater (in 1957),[7] and

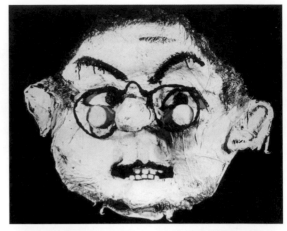

two years later he made a splash with his landmark Happening, *The Burning Building* (1959).[8]

The opulent, 6,000-seat Roxy, built in 1927, boasted a 110-foot screen and a 110-member orchestra rising from a pit,[9] while *The Burning Building* was a scruffy, anarchic love story that climaxes with the cast chasing Pasty Man (Grooms) around the handmade set until he jumps out of the eponymous house afire.[10] As the '50s turned into the '60s, with these experiences behind him and *Shoot the Moon* around the corner, the eye-filling immediacy of cinema's 24 frames per second and the kinetic physicality of live theater were already pumping through his creative bloodstream.

Red Grooms and Rudy Burckhardt,
Shoot the Moon, 1962

Georges Méliès, *A Trip to the Moon
(Le Voyage dans la Lune)*, 1902

Red Grooms and Terry Barrell
The Burning Building, 1959
13 1/2 x 8 9/16 in. / 34.3 x 21.8 cm
Photograph by John Cohen
Gift of the Collectors Committee
National Gallery of Art,
Washington 2000.135.1

There's a painting the size of a book cover, *Portrait of a Carthusian* (1446) by Petrus Christus, in New York's Metropolitan Museum of Art. Delicately rendered in oil on wood, it possesses a magnetism that far surpasses its modest scale. The anonymous, bearded, white-robed monk stares at us from a red interior where the balance of light, shadow, and perspective is so convincingly executed that he seems to physically separate, like a cutout, from the wall behind him.

As a coup de grâce, Christus has painted a faux frame around the panel and a hyperrealistic fly sitting on the frame's lower left corner. This optical trickery, a 15th-century Netherlandish version of "3-D-ing," vaporizes the fourth wall and pushes the imagery outward into our personal space. The presumably metaphorical juxtaposition between a luminous, almost beatific clerical portrait and a dissonant portent of our mortality, in the guise of a grubby bit of ordinary life, holds our imagination as much as our gaze. It is also very funny.

By acknowledging the reality on the other side of the picture plane, Christus pulls us into his world as much as the monk appears to be engaging with ours. *Portrait of a Carthusian* is not the only work of pre-Modern art to indulge in illusionistic play; it comes to mind as one of many examples of the timeless human desire to leave the role of observer and enter into a realm more beautiful, hilarious, or horrifying than the one we usually inhabit.

Petrus Christus, *Portrait of a Carthusian*, 1446,
oil on wood, 11 1/2 x 8 1/2 in.
29.2 x 21.6 cm
The Jules Bache Collection, 1949 (49.7.19)
The Metropolitan Museum of Art, New York, NY, USA Image copyright © The Metropolitan Museum of Art. Image source: Art Resource, NY

As children, we take delight in worlds in miniature — dollhouses, dioramas, puppet theaters — kingdoms we can master through our imaginations. (Conversely, to be thrust into a domain beyond our control, as witnessed by the very young Red Grooms in the pseudo-Parthenon's empty, yawning space, can be abjectly terrifying.)

Artificial environments like the Roxy Theater and the rough-and-tumble sets of *The Burning Building* and *Shoot the Moon* are also worlds in miniature, 110-foot screens

notwithstanding, for grownups to enjoy, yet the core of
their appeal lies in the same trembling wonder and fear
we experienced in childhood. To retain our humanity
means never to lose our awe at the phenomenon of
creation, or our helplessness in the face of an indifferent
universe.

The slippage between the real and unreal, darkness and
light, has been the undercurrent coursing through the art
of Red Grooms for decades. His signature walk-through
works, *City of Chicago* (1967) and *Ruckus Manhattan*
(1975), transform the viewer into a participant and even
co-creator. Marcel Duchamp's idea that the observer
completes the artwork has never been more fully, or
literally, validated:

> All in all, the creative act is not performed by
> the artist alone; the spectator brings the work in
> contact with the external world by deciphering
> and interpreting its inner qualifications and thus
> adds his contribution to the creative act.[11]

Red Grooms, *City of Chicago*, 1967

Detail from *Ruckus Manhattan,*
Woolworth Building, 1976

Red Grooms, *Keep Moving*, 2017
(detail)

The spectator wandering through a sculpto-pictorama not only "brings the work in contact with the external world by deciphering and interpreting its inner qualifications," but also acts as an ambassador from that world, injecting it with a multitude of perspectives and impressions.

Even when Grooms's artworks are intended to be simply looked at rather than walked into, their interaction with the viewer is viscerally charged, through the artist's choice of content and means of execution. The teeming genre scenes, which often push physically outward with an aggressive lurch, invariably touch on real-world experiences, no matter how exaggerated or comic they appear at first. We lean in to see more, because there is so much to see, and what we see rings true.

Despite their resistance to neat Modern or Postmodern categories, these works fall into four timeless art historical formats: painting (*Chez Red*, 2004); bas-relief (*The Big Game*, 1980-82); high relief (*Easter Parade*, 1994); and freestanding sculpture (*Joltin' Joe Takes a Swing*, 1985-88).

Echoes of Grooms's indelible encounter at the Parthenon with Jackson Pollock's all-over, agitated surface resonate throughout, with the obvious exception of the freestanding sculptures — though one, *Queen Peggy* (2004), a portrait of an imperious Peggy Guggenheim seated on a neoclassical throne — memorializes the art-world powerhouse responsible for putting Pollock on the map.

Previous page:
Red Grooms, *Joltin' Joe Takes a Swing*, 1985-88

Red Grooms, *Queen Peggy*, 2004 (detail)

19

There is a stylistic democratization at work as Grooms explores the physical anomalies of the anonymous and the famous alike with the same rapt fascination: art becomes, in its own way, the great equalizer. (It should be noted that in Grooms-World, the legendary Yankee Joe DiMaggio, whose 56-game hitting streak from 1941 still stands,[12] takes a strike.)

In paintings such as *Chez Red* (2004) and *The Funny Place* (2005), the surface is buzzing with all-over activity — the first depicting a self-named restaurant bustling with athletes, artists, snobs, and carousers; the second a jam-packed beach scene on Coney Island — as our eyes bounce from one patch of vibrant color to the next.

The commotion stirs a different reaction once Grooms revs up his 3-D-ing engines, burgeoning the crush of shapes into real space. In a bas-relief such as *Keep Moving* (2017) — a rendering of a road repair site in the middle of a busy city intersection and the inevitable traffic snarl it creates — the cars and trucks and people pebbling the surface crunch together until they seem to pop outward all at once, spontaneously capitulating to the stresses of their own inner pressure. We are lured by their toylike charm, until the sheer volume of humans and vehicles reverberates with overcompensation for the horror vacui that Grooms experienced as a child, settling into a quietly absurd sense of dread, like the one T.S. Eliot felt as he watched the crowds flow over London Bridge.[13]

The farther Grooms wrests his compositions from the flatness of the picture plane, the more dazzling, even delirious, they become. In real life, the Gothic grandeur of St. Patrick's Cathedral, rising above New York's Fifth Avenue, couldn't be more removed from the thousands of humble side streets crisscrossing the city, yet the high reliefs that Grooms wrought from these two subjects — *Easter Parade*, with its soaring, *Caligari*-esque cathedral fronted by gaily costumed crowds, and *Autumn in New York* (2017), filled with brilliantly colored leaves clinging

Previous page:
Red Grooms, *The Big Game*, 1980-82 (detail)

Red Grooms, *The Funny Place*, 2005 (detail)

23

to trees and blown across the pavement — are nonetheless equally resplendent. The first reflects a previous generation's spiritual aspirations as they persist — or dissipate — in an increasingly secularized society, while the other delights in a vestige of nature that stubbornly flourishes in an assertively urban environment. Both refuse to moralize over the implications of the imagery; they are content to indulge in the grace of taking things as they are.

Grooms's refusal to cast judgment, especially with regard to pastimes and pleasure — is elemental to the universality of his art. When people eat, they eat with gusto, mouths wide and portions gigantic; the bearded diner in *Bagels and Cream Cheese* (2011) bites into his supersized schmear with such force that he separates himself from the background, like Christus's monk, but this time literally, an actual cutout. The throw of a solitary bowler (*Strike*, 1992) is rendered with as much single-minded purposefulness, and indeed violence, as the clash of amped-up football players (*The Big Game*, 1980-82). And everywhere the city's anarchic exuberance reigns supreme, whether absorbed from street level (*Walk On By*, 2017) — or even below street level (the sewer workers painted on the underside of *Headlights*, 2002) — or from on high, far above the skyscrapers' peaks (*Manhattan Moves Up*, 2016).

The open heartedness manifest in Grooms's work — its comfort in our idiosyncrasies and empathy for our failings, cloaked in the balm of humor — carries a particular meaning in this place and time. It reminds us that our urges and desires are not appetites we harbor alone, but bonds in the humanity we share, and that to separate ourselves from the energy and irritation of others diminishes us more than we care to know.

Red Grooms, *Bagels and Cream Cheese*, 2011 (detail)

Previous page:
Red Grooms, *Easter Parade*, 1994 (detail)

Red Grooms, *Autumn in New York*, 2017 (detail)

To engage with the realms Grooms has created is to immerse ourselves in the past and the future, leaving the present aside — a void that, with any luck, only sharpens our memory and potential. For the moment, stuck as we are like Samuel Beckett's ever-hopeful Winnie, Grooms's perpetual-motion burlesques offer us more than our fair share of respite and release.[14]

Endnotes

[1] Timothy Hyman, interview with Red Grooms in *Red Grooms* (New York: Rizzoli, 2004), 105.

[2] Judd Tully, "Red Grooms has Artful Fun with High Culture...and Low," *Smithsonian*, June 1985, 106.

[3] Judith E. Stein, *Red Grooms: A Retrospective* (Philadelphia: Pennsylvania Academy of Fine Arts, 1985), 10.

[4] Ibid.

[5] Ibid.

[6] Ibid.

[7] Ibid, 32-35.

[8] Ibid.

[9] Ken Bloom, *Broadway: Its History, People, and Places, An Encyclopedia* (New York: Routledge, 2012), 463.

[10] Carter Ratcliff, *Red Grooms* (New York: Abbeville Press, 1984), 48.

[11] Marcel Duchamp, "The Creative Act" in *Salt Seller: The Writings of Marcel Duchamp*, ed. Michel Sanouillet and Elmer Peterson (New York: Oxford University Press, 1973), 140.

[12] "Longest hitting streaks in MLB history," Major League Baseball. April 11, 2019. http://mlb.com/news/longest-hitting-streaks-in-mlb-history.

[13] T.S. Eliot, *The Waste Land* (New York: Boni & Liveright, 1922), 7.

[14] Samuel Beckett, *Happy Days*, (New York: Grove Press, 1961).

Red Grooms, *Manhattan Moves Up*, 2016 (detail)

Plates

Red Grooms in collaboration with Mimi Gross and the Ruckus Construction Company
From Ruckus Manhattan, Wall Street – Newsstand, Lamppost and Bum, 1976
mixed media construction
113 x 144 x 50 in. / 287 x 365.8 x 127 cm

Exhibitions:

Ruckus Manhattan: Lower Manhattan, 88 Pine Street, New York, NY, 1975

Red Grooms and the Ruckus Construction Co. Presents Ruckus Manhattan, Marlborough Gallery, New York, NY, 1976

Ruckus Manhattan Revival, Burlington House, New York, NY, 1981

Red Grooms: Ruckus Manhattan, The Seibu Museum of Art, Tokyo, Japan, 1982

Red Grooms: Retrospective, Whitney Museum of American Art, New York, NY, 1987

Red Grooms at Grand Central Terminal, Grand Central Terminal, New York, NY, 1993

Red Grooms, Nagoya City Art Museum, Nagoya, Japan; traveled to Ashiya City Museum of Art and History, Ashiya, Japan; Mitsukoshi Museum of Art, Tokyo, Japan; and The Museum of Art, Kochi, Japan, 1993

Red Grooms, Knoxville Museum of Art, Knoxville, TN, 1997

Red Grooms, New York: 1976-2011, Marlborough Gallery, New York, NY, 2011

New York, New York, Nassau County Museum of Art, Roslyn Harbor, NY, 2017

Art in the Open: Fifty Years of Public Art in New York, Museum of the City of New York, NY, 2017-18

Red Grooms, Marlborough Gallery, New York, NY, 2021

Literature:

Ashbery, John. *Red Grooms: Ruckus Manhattan.* Tokyo: The Seibu Museum of Art, 1982.

Danto, Arthur C., Timothy Hyman, and Marco Livingston. *Red Grooms.* New York: Rizzoli, 2004.

Haskell, Barbara. Red Grooms: *Ruckus Rodeo.* New York: Harry N. Abrams, 1988.

Heartney, Eleanor, and Sarah H. Kramer. *Red Grooms.* Edited by Stephen C. Wicks. Knoxville, Tennessee: Knoxville Museum of Art, 1997.

Tully, Judd. *Red Grooms and Ruckus Manhattan.* New York: George Braziller, Inc., 1977.

Yamakawaki, Kazuo and Arthur C. Danto. *Red Grooms.* Nagoya, Japan: Nagoya City Art Museum, 1993.

Wall Street Components:
Newsstand, Lamppost and Bum are an integral component of the overall
Wall Street segment of Ruckus Manhattan which is being held together as
a single installation.

Wall Street Includes:
11 x 26 x 51 '

> Willie the Preacher exhorting the Wall Street community from the base of the statue of George
> Washington on the steps of Federal Hall
> Lunch-time revelers on the steps of Federal Hall
> The pastor of Trinity at the church door, and a bootblack at the subway entrance on Broadway
> Trinity Church and its graveyard, including the skeletons of two inhabitants: Alexander Hamilton and
> Robert Fulton
> Fire on Wall Street: Mother Bank succumbs to anarchist bomb
> Chase Manhattan Plaza including Noguchi rock garden and Dubuffet's Four Trees
> Newsstand, Lamppost and Bum

As the title [*Ruckus Manhattan*] suggests, this Grooms-eye view of Manhattan stresses the city's manic energy. Wall Street, the section of this monumental work included in this exhibition, reveals the breadth of Grooms' ambition. All the familiar landmarks are there – the Gothic spires of Trinity Church, blackened with years of soot: the neoclassical façade of that modern day temple, the New York Stock Exchange, into which one may peek for a glimpse of frantic traders: the Victorian filigree of the Woolworth Building topped by a nickel and dime dragon whose avaricious spirit rules the neighborhood.

The viewer who ventures into this labyrinth work mingles with the crush of humanity who dwell beneath these towering buildings. Vignettes focus on mini-dramas – the newsstand proprietor selling lottery tickets, a self-styled preacher railing to a motley crew of completely uninterested bystanders beneath the statue of George Washington, a businessman wrapped around a building by a gust of wind as he hurries back to the office.

In Grooms' hands, the city becomes as elastic as a bowl of Jello. Vistas expand and contract and buildings and alleyways curl to enfold the visitor as if Manhattan itself ere a living, breathing creature.

Excerpt by Eleanor Heartney from *A Grooms Eye View,* p. 4

Photo by Jacob Burckhardt, 1976

The Big Game, 1980-82
polychrome cast aluminum, edition 3 of 3
94 x 109 3/4 x 16 in. / 238.8 x 278.8 x 40.6 cm

Exhibitions:

Red Grooms: Recent Works, Marlborough Gallery, New York, NY, 1981

1988 Butler Midyear Exhibition, Butler Institute of American Art, Youngstown, OH, 1988

Red Grooms, Nagoya City Art Museum, Nagoya, Japan; traveled to Ashiya City Museum of Art and History, Ashiya, Japan; Mitsukoshi Museum of Art, Tokyo, Japan; and The Museum of Art, Kochi, Japan, 1993

Red Grooms, Knoxville Museum of Art, Knoxville, TN, 1997

Red Grooms and the Heroism of Modern Life, Palmer Museum of Art, University Park, PA, 1998

Red Grooms: Sculpture, Grounds for Sculpture, Hamilton, NJ, 2000

Red Grooms, Lord and Taylor, New York, NY, 2003

Nassau Red! Red Grooms / Ruckus in Roslyn, Nassau County Museum of Art, Roslyn Harbor, NY, 2005-6

Red Grooms, Marlborough Gallery, New York, NY, 2021

Literature:

Beardsley, John. R*ed Grooms: Sculpture*. Hamilton, NJ: Grounds for Sculpture, 2000.

Heartney, Eleanor, and Sarah H. Kramer. *Red Grooms*. Edited by Stephen C. Wicks. Knoxville, Tennessee: Knoxville Museum of Art, 1997.

Ratcliff, Carter. *Red Grooms*. New York: Abbeville Press, 1984.

Robinson, Joyce Henri. *Red Grooms and the Heroism of Modern Life*. University Park, PA: Palmer Museum of Art, 1998.

Yamakawaki, Kazuo and Arthur C. Danto. *Red Grooms*. Nagoya, Japan: Nagoya City Art Museum, 1993.

Walking the Dogs, 1981
painted canvas, papier-mâché and metal chain on wood support
36 3/4 x 20 x 22 1/2 in. / 93.3 x 50.8 x 57.1 cm

Exhibitions:

Red Grooms: Recent Works, Marlborough Gallery, NY, 1981

Red Grooms: A Retrospective 1956-1984, Pennsylvania Academy of the Fine Arts, Philadelphia, PA; traveled to Denver Art Museum, Denver, CO; Museum of Contemporary Art, Los Angeles, CA; and Tennessee State Museum, Nashville, TN, 1985

Summer Group Show 2015, Marlborough Gallery, NY, 2015

Red Grooms: Handiwork, 1955-2018, Marlborough Gallery, NY, 2018

Red Grooms, Marlborough Gallery, New York, NY, 2021

Literature:

Ratcliff, Carter. *Red Grooms*. New York: Abbeville Press, 1984.

Stein, Judith, John Ashbery, and Janet K. Cutler. *Red Grooms: A Retrospective, 1956-1984*. Philadelphia: Pennsylvania Academy of Fine Arts, 1985.

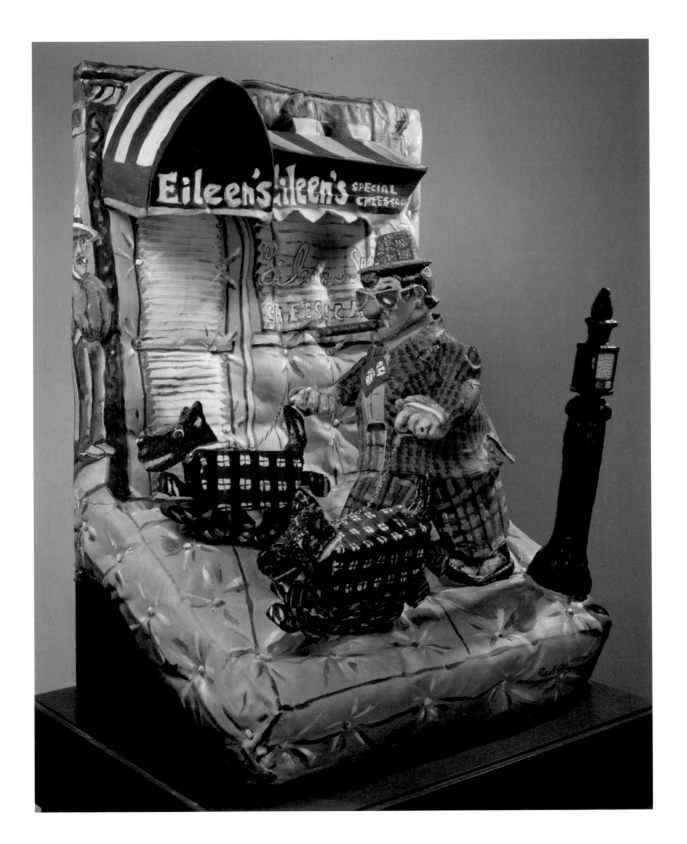

The Alley, 1984-85
mixed media construction
overall: 144 x 348 x 132 in. / 365.76 x 883.92 x 335.28 cm

Exhibitions:

Red Grooms: Recent Works, Marlborough Fine Art London, England, 1985

Red Grooms, Knoxville Museum of Art, Knoxville, TN, 1997

Red Grooms in Pursuit of Serious Fun, Contemporary Art Center of Virginia, Virginia Beach, VA, 2000

I WANT Candy: The Sweet Stuff in American Art, Hudson River Museum, Yonkers, NY, 2007

Red Grooms, New York: 1976-2011, Marlborough Gallery, New York, NY, 2011

Red Grooms: Beware a Wolf in the Alley, Marlborough Broome Street, New York, NY, 2014

New York, New York, Nassau County Museum of Art, Roslyn Harbor, NY, 2017

Literature:

Danto, Arthur C., Timothy Hyman, and Marco Livingston. *Red Grooms*. New York: Rizzoli, 2004.

Joltin' Joe Takes a Swing, 1985-88
acrylic on carved wood construction
61 x 62 x 62 in. / 154.9 x 157.5 x 157.5 cm

Exhibitions:

Red Grooms: Tourist Traps and Other Places, Marlborough Gallery, New York, NY, 1990

Red Grooms, Nagoya City Art Museum, Nagoya, Japan; traveled to Ashiya City Museum of Art and History, Ashiya, Japan; Mitsukoshi Museum of Art, Tokyo, Japan; and The Museum of Art, Kochi, Japan, 1993

Red Grooms: Sculpture, Grounds for Sculpture, Hamilton, NJ, 2000

Group Sculpture Exhibition, Marlborough Gallery, New York, NY, 2001

Red Grooms, Lord and Taylor, New York, NY, 2003

Nassau Red! Red Grooms / Ruckus in Roslyn, Nassau County Museum of Art, Roslyn Harbor, NY, 2005-6

Red Grooms, Marlborough Gallery, New York, NY, 2021

Literature:

Beardsley, John. *Red Grooms: Sculpture*. Hamilton, NJ: Grounds for Sculpture, 2000.

Danto, Arthur C., Timothy Hyman, and Marco Livingston. *Red Grooms*. New York: Rizzoli, 2004.

Yamakawaki, Kazuo and Arthur C. Danto. *Red Grooms*. Nagoya, Japan: Nagoya City Art Museum, 1993.

Strike, 1992
mixed media construction
31 1/2 x 73 1/2 x 49 1/2 in. / 80 x 186.7 x 125.7 cm

Exhibitions:

Red Grooms, Nagoya City Art Museum, Nagoya, Japan; traveled to Ashiya City Museum of Art and History, Ashiya, Japan; Mitsukoshi Museum of Art, Tokyo, Japan; and The Museum of Art, Kochi, Japan, 1993

Red Grooms, Knoxville Museum of Art, Knoxville, TN, 1997

Red Grooms: Sculpture, Grounds for Sculpture, Hamilton, NJ, 2000

Nassau Red! Red Grooms / Ruckus in Roslyn, Nassau County Museum of Art, Roslyn Harbor, NY, 2005-6

Red Grooms, Marlborough Gallery, New York, NY, 2021

Literature:

Beardsley, John. *Red Grooms: Sculpture*. Hamilton, NJ: Grounds for Sculpture, 2000.

Danto, Arthur C., Timothy Hyman, and Marco Livingston. *Red Grooms*. New York: Rizzoli, 2004.

Heartney, Eleanor, and Sarah H. Kramer. *Red Grooms*. Edited by Stephen C. Wicks. Knoxville, Tennessee: Knoxville Museum of Art, 1997.

Yamakawaki, Kazuo and Arthur C. Danto. *Red Grooms*. Nagoya, Japan: Nagoya City Art Museum, 1993.

Easter Parade, 1994
acrylic and mixed media construction
80 x 87 x 34 in. / 203.2 x 221 x 86.4 cm

Exhibitions:

Red Grooms: New York Stories, Marlborough Gallery, New York, NY, 1995

Red Grooms in Pursuit of Serious Fun, Contemporary Art Center of Virginia, Virginia Beach, VA, 2000

Town and Country: In Pursuit of Life's Pleasures, Nassau County Museum of Fine Art, Roslyn Harbor, NY, 1996

Red Grooms, Knoxville Museum of Art, Knoxville, TN, 1997

Red Grooms, Mary Brogan Museum of Art and Science, Tallahassee, FL, 2001

Red Grooms, Lord and Taylor, New York, NY, 2003

Nassau Red! Red Grooms / Ruckus in Roslyn, Nassau County Museum of Art, Roslyn Harbor, NY, 2005-6

Red Grooms: What's the Ruckus, Brattleboro Museum & Art Center, Brattleboro, VT, 2013

Red Grooms, New York: 1976-2011, Marlborough Gallery, New York, NY, 2011

Red Grooms, Marlborough Gallery, New York, NY, 2021

Literature:

Danto, Arthur C., Timothy Hyman, and Marco Livingston. *Red Grooms.* New York: Rizzoli, 2004.

Heartney, Eleanor, and Sarah H. Kramer. *Red Grooms.* Edited by Stephen C. Wicks. Knoxville, Tennessee: Knoxville Museum of Art, 1997.

The Duck House, 1994
mixed media construction
56 1/2 x 58 1/2 x 28 in. / 143.5 x 148.6 x 71.1 cm

Exhibitions:

Figures de l'Art d'Aujourd'hui, Galerie Marwan Hoss, Paris, France, 1994

Red Grooms: New York Stories, Marlborough Gallery, New York, NY, 1995

A Ruckus on Paper and Other Constructions, McNay Art Museum, San Antonio, TX, 1997

Adventures Past and Present with Red Grooms, Irving Galleries, Palm Beach, FL, 2004

Nassau Red! Red Grooms / Ruckus in Roslyn, Nassau County Museum of Art, Roslyn Harbor, NY, 2005-6

Red Grooms, New York: 1976-2011, Marlborough Gallery, New York, NY, 2011

Red Grooms: What's the Ruckus, Brattleboro Museum & Art Center, Brattleboro, VT, 2013

Red Grooms, Marlborough Gallery, New York, NY, 2021

The Plaza, 1995
acrylic and mixed media construction
69 1/2 x 91 1/4 x 18 in. / 176.5 x 231.8 x 45.7 cm

Exhibitions:

Red Grooms: New York Stories, Marlborough Gallery, New York, NY, 1995

Group Show, Marlborough, New York, NY, 1995-6

Red Grooms and the Heroism of Modern Life, Palmer Museum of Art, University Park, PA, 1998

Red Grooms in Pursuit of Serious Fun, Contemporary Art Center of Virginia, Virginia Beach, VA, 2000

Red Grooms, Mary Brogan Museum of Art and Science, Tallahassee, FL, 2001

Red Grooms, Lord and Taylor, New York, NY, 2003

Nassau Red! Red Grooms / Ruckus in Roslyn, Nassau County Museum of Art, Roslyn Harbor, NY, 2005-6

Red Grooms: What's the Ruckus, Brattleboro Museum & Art Center, Brattleboro, VT, 2013

New York, New York, Nassau County Museum of Art, Roslyn Harbor, NY, 2017

Red Grooms, Marlborough Gallery, New York, NY, 2021

Study for Tattoo Parlor, 1998
acrylic on board
53 x 40 in. / 134.6 x 101.6 cm

Exhibitions:

Red Grooms: peintures et sculptures, Galerie Patrice Trigano, Paris, France, 2000

Red Grooms, New York: 1976-2011, Marlborough Gallery, New York, NY, 2011

Red Grooms, Marlborough Gallery, New York, NY, 2021

Headlights, 2002
acrylic on mixed media construction
22 1/8 x 22 x 11 1/2 in. / 56.2 x 55.9 x 29.2 cm

Exhibitions:

Red Grooms: New Works in Wood, Marlborough Gallery, New York, NY, 2004

Red Grooms: Paris–New York, Galerie Patrice Trigano, Paris, France, 2005

Red Grooms, Russeck Gallery, Palm Beach, FL, 2007

Red Grooms, New York: 1976-2011, Marlborough Gallery, New York, NY, 2011

Red Grooms: Handiwork, 1955-2018, Marlborough Gallery, New York, NY, 2018

Red Grooms, Marlborough Gallery, New York, NY, 2021

Shave and a Haircut, Six Dollars, 2003
acrylic on wood construction
52 x 68 x 14 in. / 132.1 x 172.7 x 35.6 cm

Exhibitions:

Summer Show, Marlborough Gallery, New York, NY, 2004

Red Grooms: New Works in Wood, Marlborough Gallery, New York, NY, 2004

Red Grooms: What's the Ruckus, Brattleboro Museum & Art Center, Brattleboro, VT, 2013

Red Grooms, Marlborough Gallery, New York, NY, 2021

Literature:

Danto, Arthur C., Timothy Hyman, and Marco Livingston. Red Grooms. New York: Rizzoli, 2004.

Lui's Store, 2002
acrylic on wood construction
37 3/4 x 31 1/4 x 15 3/4 in. / 95.9 x 79.4 x 40 cm

Exhibitions:

Red Grooms: New Works in Wood, Marlborough Gallery, New York, NY, 2004

Red Grooms: Paris–New York, Galerie Patrice Trigano, Paris, France, 2005

Sobre el Humor, Galería Marlborough, Madrid, Spain, 2007

Winter Group Exhibition, Marlborough Gallery, New York, NY, 2007-8

Summer Group Exhibition, Marlborough Gallery, New York, NY, 2008

Summer Exhibition, Marlborough Gallery, New York, NY, 2015

Summer Group Show, Marlborough Gallery, New York, NY, 2016

Red Grooms, Marlborough Gallery, New York, NY, 2021

Deli, 2003
ink and crayon on paper
22 1/2 x 30 in. / 57.2 x 76.2 cm

Exhibitions:

Red Grooms, Marlborough Gallery, New York, NY, 2021

Following page:
Chez Red, 2004
latex and acrylic on paper mounted on panel
107 x 156 in. / 271.8 x 395.6 cm

Exhibitions:

Red Grooms: New Works in Wood, Marlborough Gallery, New York, NY, 2004

Nassau Red! Red Grooms / Ruckus in Roslyn, Nassau County Museum of Art, Roslyn Harbor, New York, NY, 2005-6

Red Grooms, Marlborough Gallery, New York, NY, 2021

Queen Peggy, 2004
oil paint over aluminum construction, edition 1 of 2
45 1/4 x 43 x 31 1/2 in. / 115 x 109.2 x 80 cm

Exhibitions:

Red Grooms: New Works in Wood, Marlborough Gallery, New York, NY, 2004

Nassau Red! Red Grooms / Ruckus in Roslyn, Nassau County Museum of Art, Roslyn Harbor, NY, 2005-6

Sculpture, Marlborough, New York, NY, 2005

Red Grooms and Andrew Saftel, Cumberland Gallery, Nashville, TN, 2010

Red Grooms, Marlborough Gallery, New York, NY, 2021

The Funny Place, 2005
oil on canvas
50 x 40 in. / 127 x 101.6 cm

Exhibitions:

Red Grooms: Recent Paintings, Marlborough Gallery, New York, NY, 2007

Red Grooms, New York: 1976-2011, Marlborough Gallery, New York, NY, 2011

Red Grooms: What's the Ruckus, Brattleboro Museum & Art Center, Brattleboro, VT, 2013

Coney Island: Visions of an American Dreamland, Wadsworth Atheneum, Hartford, CT, United States. Traveled to Brooklyn Museum, Brooklyn, NY, United States, McNay Art Museum, San Antonio, TX, United States, 2014-16

Red Grooms: Traveling Correspondent, Memphis Brooks Museum of Art, Memphis, TN, 2016

Red Grooms, Marlborough Gallery, New York, NY, 2021

Literature:

Jaffee Frank, Robin. *Coney Island: Visions of an American Dreamland*, 1861-2008. Hartford, CT: Wadsworth Atheneum Museum of Art, 2015.

Pacini, Marina. *Red Grooms: Traveling Correspondent*. Memphis, TN: Memphis Brooks Museum of Art, 2016.

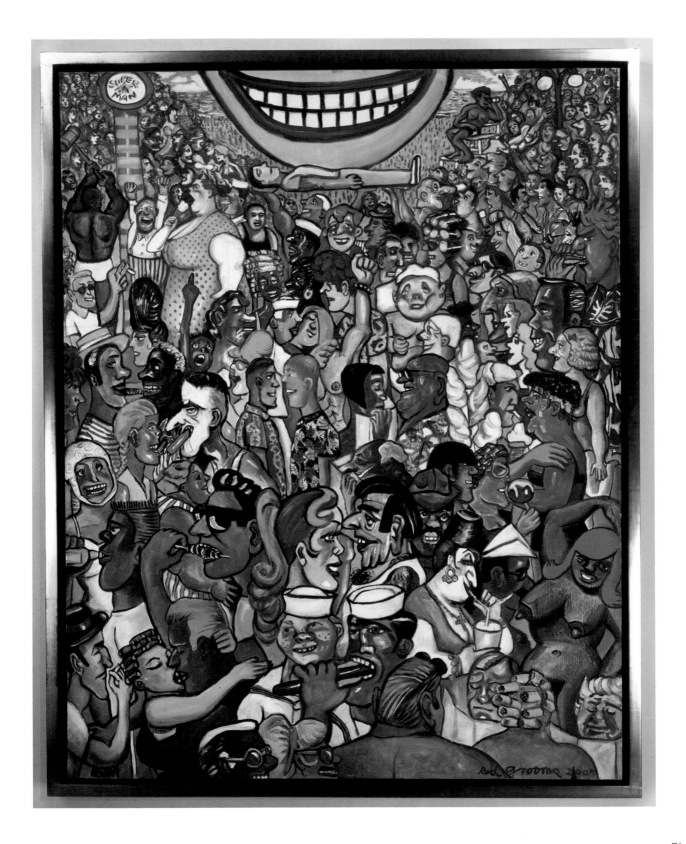

Eggs Over Midnight, 2007
oil on canvas
14 x 14 in. / 35.6 x 35.6 cm

Exhibitions:

Red Grooms: Recent Paintings, Marlborough Gallery, New York, NY, 2007

Red Grooms, New York: 1976-2011, Marlborough Gallery, New York, NY, 2011

Red Grooms, Marlborough Gallery, New York, NY, 2021

The Client, 2007
oil on canvas
14 x 14 in. / 35.6 x 35.6 cm

Exhibitions:

Red Grooms: Recent Paintings, Marlborough Gallery, New York, NY, 2007

Red Grooms, New York: 1976-2011, Marlborough Gallery, New York, NY, 2011

Red Grooms, Marlborough Gallery, New York, NY, 2021

Mr. Bones, 2011
tempera and acrylic on construction mounted on board
60 x 40 x 3 in. / 152.4 x 101.6 x 7.6 cm

Exhibitions:

Red Grooms, New York: 1976-2011, Marlborough Gallery, New York, NY, 2011

Red Grooms, Marlborough Gallery, New York, NY, 2021

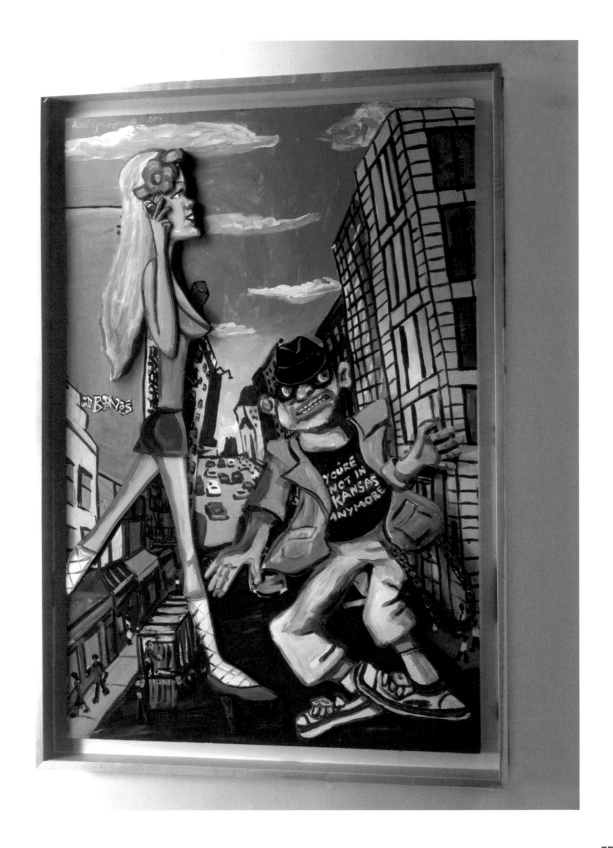

Bagels and Cream Cheese, 2011
acrylic construction mounted on board
60 x 40 x 2 in. / 152.4 x 101.6 x 5.1 cm

Exhibitions:

Red Grooms: Handiwork 1955 to the present, Marlborough Gallery, New York, NY, 2018

Red Grooms, Marlborough Gallery, New York, NY, 2021

Lil' Red on Broome Street, 2014
charcoal, acrylic and crayon on paper
33 3/4 x 35 1/2 in. / 85.7 x 90.2 cm

Exhibitions:

Beware a Wolf in the Alley, Marlborough Gallery, New York, NY, 2014

Red Grooms, Marlborough Gallery, New York, NY, 2021

Harbor Lights, 2016
acrylic, ink and epoxy mounted on wood
40 1/2 x 61 1/2 x 5 1/4 in. / 104.8 x 156.2 x 14.6 cm

Exhibitions:

Red Grooms: New York On My Mind, Marlborough Gallery, New York, NY, 2017

Red Grooms, Marlborough Gallery, New York, NY, 2021

Following page:
The Strand, 2015-17
acrylic, ink, mixed media and epoxy mounted on wood
73 1/3 x 118 1/2 x 9 in. / 186.3 x 301 x 22.9 cm

Exhibitions:
Red Grooms: New York On My Mind, Marlborough Gallery, New York, NY, 2017
Red Grooms, Marlborough Gallery, New York, NY, 2021

Vertigo, 2016
acrylic, ink, mixed media and epoxy mounted on wood
33 x 24 x 5 in. / 83.8 x 60.9 x 17.8 cm

Exhibitions:

Red Grooms: New York On My Mind, Marlborough Gallery, New York, NY, 2017

Summer Group Show, Marlborough Gallery, New York, NY, 2017

Red Grooms, Marlborough Gallery, New York, NY, 2021

Night Falls on Canal Street, 2016
acrylic, ink, mixed media and epoxy mounted on wood
40 1/2 x 28 1/4 x 5 in. / 102.9 x 71.8 x 12.7 cm

Exhibitions:

Red Grooms: New York On My Mind, Marlborough Gallery, New York, NY, 2017

Red Grooms, Marlborough Gallery, New York, NY, 2021

Manhattan Moves Up, 2016
acrylic, ink, mixed media and epoxy mounted on wood
29 x 23 x 5 3/4 in. / 73.7 x 58.4 x 14.6 cm

Exhibitions:

Red Grooms: New York On My Mind, Marlborough Gallery, New York, NY, 2017

Red Grooms, Marlborough Gallery, New York, NY, 2021

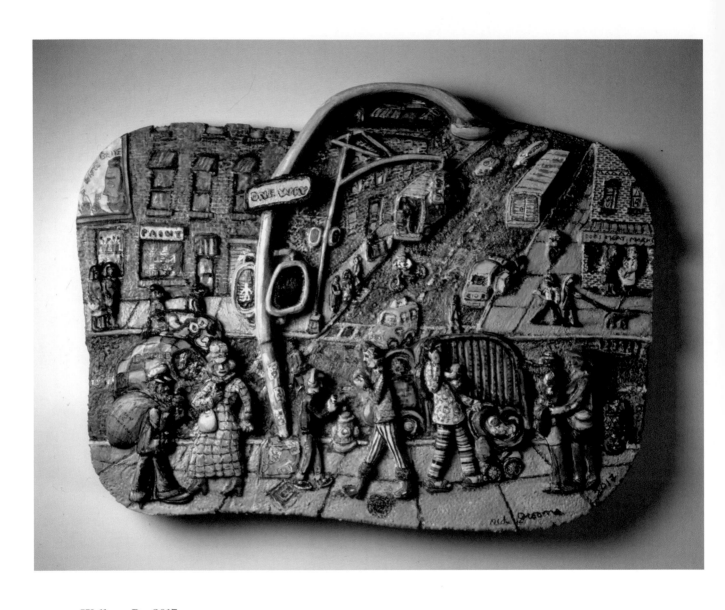

Walk on By, 2017
acrylic, ink, mixed media and epoxy mounted on wood
34 x 44 1/2 x 4 1/2 in. / 87.6 x 114.9 x 11.4 cm

Exhibitions:

Red Grooms: New York On My Mind, Marlborough Gallery, New York, NY, 2017

Red Grooms, Marlborough Gallery, New York, NY, 2021

Following page:
Autumn in New York, 2017
acrylic, ink, mixed media and epoxy mounted on wood
37 x 61 1/2 x 14 1/2 in. / 94 x 156.2 x 36.8 cm

Exhibitions:
Red Grooms: New York On My Mind, Marlborough Gallery, New York, NY, 2017
Red Grooms, Marlborough Gallery, New York, NY, 2021

A View of the Sea, 2017
acrylic on paper
51 1/4 x 65 1/4 in. / 130.2 x 165.7 cm

Exhibition:

Red Grooms: New York On My Mind, Marlborough Gallery, New York, NY, 2017

Red Grooms: Handiwork, 1955-2018, Marlborough Gallery, New York, NY, 2018

Red Grooms, Marlborough Gallery, New York, NY, 2021

Keep Moving, 2017
acrylic, ink, mixed media and epoxy mounted on wood
35 1/2 x 48 x 10 3/4 in. / 90.17 x 121.9 x 27.31 cm

Exhibitions:

Red Grooms: New York On My Mind, Marlborough Gallery, New York, NY, 2017

Summer Group Show, Marlborough Gallery, New York, NY, 2017

Red Grooms, Marlborough Gallery, New York, NY, 2021

Room with A View, 2017
acrylic, ink, mixed media and epoxy mounted on wood
96 x 29 1/2 x 4 in. / 243.8 x 74.9 x 10.2 cm

Exhibitions:

Red Grooms: New York On My Mind, Marlborough Gallery, New York, NY, 2017

Group Exhibition, Marlborough Gallery, New York, NY, 2018

Red Grooms, Marlborough Gallery, New York, NY, 2021

Museum and Public Collections

Addison Gallery of American Art, Phillips Academy, Andover, Massachusetts

Allen Memorial Art Museum, Oberlin, Ohio

Arkansas Art Center, Little Rock, Arkansas

The Art Institute of Chicago, Chicago, Illinois

Brooklyn Museum of Art, Brooklyn, New York

The Butler Institute of American Art, Youngstown, Ohio

Carnegie Museum of Art, Pittsburgh, Pennsylvania

Cheekwood Botanical Garden and Museum of Art, Nashville, Tennessee

Chrysler Museum of Art, Norfolk, Virginia

The Cleveland Museum of Art, Cleveland, Ohio

Colby College Museum of Art, Waterville, Maine

Currier Museum of Art, Manchester, New Hampshire

Dallas Museum of Art, Dallas, Texas

Delaware Art Museum, Wilmington, Delaware

Denver Art Museum, Denver, Colorado

Des Moines Art Center, Des Moines, Iowa

Everson Museum of Art, Syracuse, New York

Fine Arts Museums of San Francisco, San Francisco, California

Hirschhorn Museum and Sculpture Garden, Washington, D.C.

Hudson River Museum, Yonkers, New York

Hunter Museum of American Art, Chattanooga, Tennessee

Iwaki City Art Museum, Iwaki, Fukushima, Japan

Kemper Museum of Contemporary Art, Kansas City, Missouri

Memphis Brooks Museum of Art, Memphis, Tennessee

Metropolitan Museum of Art, New York, New York

Mint Museum, Charlotte, North Carolina

Modern Art Museum of Fort Worth, Fort Worth, Texas

Moderna Museet, Stockholm, Sweden

Red Grooms, *Strike*, 1992 (detail)

The Morgan Library and Museum, New York, New York

Museo de Arte Contemporaneo, Caracas, Venezuela

Museum of Art, Kochi, Japan

Museum of Art Fort Lauderdale, Fort Lauderdale, Florida

Museum of Contemporary Art, Chicago, Illinois

Museum of Modern Art, New York

Museum of the Moving Image, Queens, New York

Nagoya City Art Museum, Nagoya, Japan

National Portrait Gallery, Smithsonian Institute, Washington D.C.

National Gallery of Art, Washington, D.C.

New Jersey State Museum, Trenton, New Jersey

New School Art Center, New York, New York

New York Historical Society, New York, New York

Northern Kentucky University, Newport, Kentucky

Norton Gallery and School of Art, West Palm Beach, Florida

Palmer Museum of Art, Pennsylvania State University, University Park, Pennsylvania

Pennsylvania Academy of Fine Arts, Philadelphia, Pennsylvania

Philadelphia Museum of Art, Philadelphia, Pennsylvania

Smart Museum of Art, The University of Chicago, Chicago, Illinois

Solomon R. Guggenheim Museum, New York, New York

Smithsonian American Art Museum, Washington, D.C.

Southern Illinois University Museum, Southern Illinois University, Carbondale, Illinois

Vera List Center for Art and Politics, The New School, New York, New York

Whitney Museum of American Art, New York, New York

Yale University Art Gallery, New Haven, Connecticut

Red Grooms, *The Strand*, 2015-17 (detail)

Abbreviated Bibliography

Alexander, Brooke, and Virginia Cowles, et al. *Red Grooms: A Catalogue Raisonné of His Graphic Work 1957-1981.* Nashville: The Fine Arts Center, Cheekwood, 1981.

Ashbery, John. "Painting the Town Red." *Newsweek*, April 1981.

Ashbery, John. *Red Grooms: Ruckus Manhattan.* Tokyo: The Seibu Museum of Art, 1982.

Beardsley, John. *Red Grooms: Sculpture.* Hamilton, NJ: Grounds for Sculpture, 2000.

Belloli, Jay, and Koshalek, Richard. *The Great American Rodeo.* Fort Worth: Christian University Press for Fort Worth Art Museum, 1976.

Bland, Bartholomew F. *Red Grooms: In the Studio.* Yonkers, NY: Hudson River Museum, 2008.

Buckley, Laurene. *Red Grooms: A Personal History of Art.* New Britain, CT: New Britain Museum of American Art, 1997.

Butler, Susan L. *Late Twentieth Century Art from the Sydney and Frances Lewis Foundation.* Anderson Gallery, Richmond, VA: Virginia Commonwealth University, 1978.

Canaday, John. "An Evening with Red Grooms." *Smithsonian Associate* 10, February/March 1982.

Cate, Phillip Dennis. *The Ruckus World of Red Grooms.* Rutgers, NJ: Berkowitz Press for Rutgers University Art Gallery, 1973.

Danto, Arthur C., Timothy Hyman, and Marco Livingstone. *Red Grooms.* New York: Rizzoli, 2004.

Dervaux, Isabelle. *The Human Comedy: Portraits by Red Grooms.* Katonah, NY.: Katonah Museum of Art, 2003.

Glueck, Grace. "Odd Man Out: Red Grooms, the Ruckus Kid." *Artnews* 72, December 1973.

Grooms, Red and David Shapiro. *Red Grooms: New York Stories.* New York: Marlborough Gallery, 1995.

Grooms, Red and Judd Tully. *Have Brush Will Travel: Red Grooms' Watercolor World.* New York: Marlborough Gallery, 1993.

Grooms, Red and Lysiane Luong. *Red Grooms, New York: 1976-2011.* New York: Marlborough Gallery, 2011.

Grooms, Red. Interview by Paul Cummings. *Archives of American Art Oral History Program.* March 4 – 8, 1974.

Grooms, Red. *Public Works, Private Patrons: Images of Modern Times by Red Grooms.* Tampa, FL: Tampa Museum, 1983.

Halpern, Nora, and Barbara Freeman. *Target: Red Grooms!* Malibu, CA: Frederick R. Weissman Museum of Art, Pepperdine University, 1994.

Haskell, Barbara. *Red Grooms: Ruckus Rodeo.* New York: Harry N. Abrams, 1988.

Heartney, Eleanor, and Sarah H. Kramer. *Red Grooms.* Edited by Stephen C. Wicks. Knoxville, Tennessee: Knoxville Museum of Art, 1997.

Hughes, Robert. "Gorgeous Parody." *Time*, January 1976.

Red Grooms, *The Duck House*, 1994
(detail)

Kaprow, Allan. *Assemblage, Environments and Happenings.* New York: Harry N. Abrams, 1966.

Kardon, Janet, and Marincola, Paula. *Red Grooms' Philadelphia Cornucopia and Other Sculpto-Pictoramas.* Philadelphia: Institute of Contemporary Art, University of Pennsylvania, 1982.

Knestrick, Walter G. *Red Grooms: The Graphic Work.* New York: Harry N. Abrams, 2001.

Myers, John Bernard. *The Poets of the New York School.* Philadelphia: University of Pennsylvania Graduate School of Fine Arts, 1969.

Nadel, Dan. *Red Grooms Drawings: 1955 – 1965.* New York: Marlborough Gallery, 2018.

Naumann, Francis. "The Ruckus World of Red Grooms." *Artforum* 12, March 1974.

Pacini, Marina. *Red Grooms: Traveling Correspondent.* Memphis, TN: Memphis Brooks Museum of Art, 2016.

Ratcliff, Carter. *Red Grooms.* New York: Abbeville Press, 1984.

Richard, Paul. *Red Grooms, A Survey of His Graphic Work 1957-1985.* Washington, D.C.: Federal Reserve Board, Fine Arts Programs, 1990.

Robinson, Joyce Henri. *Red Grooms and the Heroism of Modern Life.* University Park, PA: Palmer Museum of Art, 1998.

Rose, Barbara. "Raucous, Ruckus World of Red Grooms." *Vogue* 166, July 1976.

Schwartz, Constance, and Franklin Perrell. *Nassau Red! Red Grooms / Ruckus in Roslyn.* Roslyn Harbor, NY: The Nassau County Museum of Art, 2005.

Stein, Judith, John Ashbery, and Janet K. Cutler. *Red Grooms: A Retrospective, 1956-1984.* Philadelphia: Pennsylvania Academy of Fine Arts, 1985.

Strand, Mark, and Red Grooms (illustrator). *Rembrandt Takes a Walk.* New York: Potter Style, 1987.

Strasser, Todd. "Interview with Red Grooms." *Ocular* 4, Winter 1979.

Swenson, G.R. "Reviews and Previews: New Names This Month: Red Grooms." *Artnews* 62, October 1963.

Talalay, Marjorie, William Olander, and Mark Gottlieb. *Red Grooms' Welcome to Cleveland.* Cleveland: The New Gallery of Contemporary Art, 1983.

Tully, Judd. "Way Down East, Red Grooms' Monument to D. W. Griffith." *Horizon Magazine* 22, August 1979.

Tully, Judd. *Red Grooms and Ruckus Manhattan.* New York: George Braziller, 1977.

Tully, Judd. *Ruckus Manhattan.* New York: Creative Time, 1975.

Walker, Celia, Christine Kreyling, and Rusty Freeman. *Red Grooms: What's All the Ruckus About?* Nashville, TN: Cheekwood Botanical Garden and Museum of Art, 1995.

Yamawaki, Kazuo, and Arthur C. Danto. *Red Grooms.* Nagoya, Japan: Nagoya City Art Museum, 1993.

Yau, John. *The Private World of Red Grooms.* New York: Tibor de Nagy Gallery, 2004.

Carnegie International Exhibition. Pittsburgh: Museum of Art, Carnegie Institute, 1982.

Red Grooms: Abril, 1974. Caracas: Museo de Arte Comtemporaneo, 1974.

Red Grooms à Paris. Paris: Galerie Roger d'Amécourt, 1977.

Red Grooms and Ruckus Manhattan. New York: George Braziller, 1977.

Red Grooms Extravaganza. Raleigh: North Carolina Museum of Art, 1983.

Red Grooms: Œuvres Récentes. Paris: FIAC, 1990.

Red Grooms. Caracas, Venezuela: Museo de Arte Contemporaneo, 1974.

The Early Sixties: Red Grooms. New York: Allan Frumkin Gallery, 1983.

Red Grooms, *The Strand*, 2015-17 (detail)

Marlborough Catalogues

1976
Red Grooms and the Ruckus Construction Co. Present Ruckus Manhattan. New York: Marlborough Gallery, 1976.

1981
Red Grooms: Recent Works. New York: Marlborough Gallery, 1981.

1984
Red Grooms: Recent Works. New York: Marlborough Gallery, 1984.

1987
Red Grooms: Recent Paintings, Sculptures, and Drawings. New York: Marlborough Gallery, 1987.

1989
Traveling with Red Grooms. New York: Marlborough Gallery, 1989.

1990
Red Grooms: Tourist Traps and Other Places. New York: Marlborough Gallery, 1990.

1992
Red Grooms: New Works. New York: Marlborough Gallery, 1992.

1997
Red Grooms: Works on Paper. New York: Marlborough Gallery, 1997.

1999
Red Grooms: New Works. New York: Marlborough Gallery, 1999.

2002
Red Grooms: Recent Works. New York: Marlborough Gallery, 2002.
Red Grooms: Torn from the Pages. New York: Marlborough Gallery, 2002.

2004
Red Grooms: New Works in Wood. New York: Marlborough Gallery, 2004.

2007
Red Grooms: Recent Paintings. New York: Marlborough Gallery, 2007.

2009
Red Grooms: Dancing. New York: Marlborough Gallery, 2009.

2012
Red Grooms: Torn from the Pages. New York: Marlborough Gallery, 2012.

2014
Torn from the Pages II. New York: Marlborough Gallery, 2014.
Beware a Wolf in the Alley. New York: Marlborough Gallery, 2014.

2017
Red Grooms: New York On My Mind. New York: Marlborough Gallery, 2017.

Red Grooms, *The Plaza*, 1995 (detail)

Illustration Index

Red Grooms, *Easter Parade*, 1994 (detail)